BE the CHANGE

Dedicated to the children of the world in the hope
that they will, through personal change, be the catalyst
to steer the world on the path to sanity
—A. G.

To Taru Om-Arun Bakshi, my son and greatest change
—B. H.

To my husband, Chris
—E. T.

ATHENEUM BOOKS FOR YOUNG READERS
An imprint of Simon & Schuster Children's Publishing Division
1230 Avenue of the Americas, New York, New York 10020
Text copyright © 2016 by Arun Gandhi and Bethany Hegedus
Illustrations copyright © 2016 by Evan Turk
ATHENEUM BOOKS FOR YOUNG READERS is a registered trademark of Simon & Schuster, Inc.
Atheneum logo is a trademark of Simon & Schuster, Inc.
For information about special discounts for bulk purchases, please contact
Simon & Schuster Special Sales at 1-866-506-1949 or business@simonandschuster.com.
The Simon & Schuster Speakers Bureau can bring authors to your live event.
For more information or to book an event, contact the Simon & Schuster Speakers Bureau
at 1-866-248-3049 or visit our website at www.simonspeakers.com.
Book design by Ann Bobco • The text for this book is set in Bernhard Modern BT.
The illustrations for this book are rendered in watercolor, paper collage, cotton fabric, cotton, gouache, white china marker,
colored drawing pencils, and embroidery thread. • Manufactured in China
0616 SCP • First Edition • 10 9 8 7 6 5 4 3 2 1
Library of Congress Cataloging-in-Publication Data
Gandhi, Arun.
Be the change : a grandfather Gandhi story / Arun Gandhi and Bethany Hegedus ; illustrated by Evan Turk. —
First edition.   pages cm
ISBN 978-1-4814-4265-7 (hardcover)—ISBN 978-1-4814-4266-4 (eBook)
1. Gandhi, Mahatma, 1869–1948—Juvenile literature. 2. Gandhi, Arun—Juvenile literature.
3. Pacifists—India—Biography—Juvenile literature. 4. Statesmen—India—Biography—Juvenile literature.
I. Hegedus, Bethany. II. Turk, Evan, illustrator. III. Title.
DS481.G3G184 2016   954.03′5092—dc23   [B]   2015015310

BE the CHANGE

A Grandfather Gandhi Story

Arun Gandhi and Bethany Hegedus

Illustrated by Evan Turk

atheneum

ATHENEUM BOOKS FOR YOUNG READERS

New York   London   Toronto   Sydney   New Delhi

The world knows him as the Mahatma,
Great Soul.
To me, he is Grandfather.

Life at the Sevagram ashram, Grandfather's service village, revolved around the sun. Before daybreak, we left our beds. All three hundred and fifty followers gathered for the morning prayer meeting. Peace descended on us like the rays of the sun. All religions were welcome.

The purpose of ashram life was to live simply and nonviolently. Each day was filled, from sunrise to sunset, with service. The ashram worked as one: washing clothes, planting vegetables, picking fruit, spinning yarn— anything that needed doing was done for the good of all. Grandfather had dubbed our work "Experiments in Truth."

There were eleven
vows of ashram living.
The one I found the
hardest was the vow not
to waste.

And it was an important one, a cornerstone of Grandfather's teachings. I wasn't sure how not wasting food or other items made life nonviolent, but I did my best to follow the path put before me. Bapuji said I would understand in time, but I had already lived at Sevagram for more than a year.

Soon, Grandfather asked
that I accompany him to Poona. I
was happy to get the break from ashram
life, from waking early and working hard.
But at the Nature Cure Clinic our routine
was much the same: the same vows, the same
self-discipline.

When Grandfather talked, thousands came,
overflowing the gardens. People young and old
spilled into the streets.

I stood with them and listened as he spoke about
Satyagraha, passive nonviolence. "When nonviolence
is accepted as the law of life, it must pervade the whole
being and not be applied to isolated acts," Bapuji said.

How was I to understand that? It hurt my head to even
think about.

Yet when Grandfather spoke, something in me stilled,
even if afterward my thoughts grew cloudy.

One afternoon on my way home from lessons,
I'd had enough. As I walked, I tossed my nubby
pencil in the air, tired of my vow not to waste,
tired of not understanding. It bounced into the grass.
I left it there. On purpose.

That evening, I asked Bapuji for a new pencil.

"This morning you had what appeared to be a perfectly good pencil," Grandfather said.

"It was too small. I threw it away," I argued. I didn't share what I was really thinking: I was a Gandhi—didn't I deserve a new pencil?

"It was not too small this morning." Grandfather smiled his toothless grin. "And what of your vow?"

"The one not to waste?" I stared at my sandaled feet.

"A vow is a promise to yourself before it is one to others."

"Why is a nubby pencil so important?" I asked.

"It is not the pencil, but you, that is important." Bapuji patted my shoulder.

Bapuji was talking in riddles. Why wasn't there a simple explanation?

He walked me to the door. "You will have to go and look for it."

Would I really have to search for a nub of a pencil? "But it's after dusk."

"Good thinking, Arun. You will need a torch." He handed me a flashlight and pointed me toward the night.

I set off into the dark. My face burned with shame. Grandfather had already taught me so much, and here I had more to learn. I was a disappointment—to him, to myself.

I retraced my steps. Past the bench with the broken leg. Past a pack of stray dogs. I stopped when I came to the scrubby grass that I'd cut across hours earlier.

Kneeling, I ran my fingers through the coarse stalks. Nothing.

Above, the stars seemed to mock me. *Find it, find it,* they twinkled, taunting.

Finally, after hours of searching, I found it. I stuffed the pencil in my pocket and trudged back to Grandfather's cottage.

"Did you recover the pencil?" Bapuji asked when I returned.

I had—but I still hadn't discovered what waste and nonviolence had to do with each other. Or what they had to do with me.

That night I wrestled with my thoughts. How could throwing away a pencil hurt anyone? It made no sense. Why couldn't I understand?

We returned to Sevagram.
There, Grandfather set out
to teach me the deeper meaning
of the rule not to waste just as
monsoon season had come.

The skies erupted. For days on
end, the rains beat the dry, cracked
ground. The earth became messy and
muddy as I struggled with how waste and
violence were connected.

Grandfather sat with me for
an hour a day, as busy as he was.
"Waste *is* a violent action.
When resources are low, people
hoard. Those who are forced to
do without may eventually strike
out. Fighting occurs," he said.
"Did you want any of that when
you threw away your pencil?"

I didn't. Is this why we spun?
Why we made our own cloth?

Grandfather suggested I make a tree of violence, with violence as the trunk and physical violence and passive violence, the kind that looks like it hurts no one, as the branches.

"Before you act, think how it would affect others," he said. "Who would it hurt? You? Someone else? The earth? Does hurting the earth hurt us?"

Together we created a tree and pasted it on the wall. Each day, I added my thoughts and actions to it.

Grandfather would come by my hut, and he'd watch my tree grow. When I wasn't sure where to place something, he helped me decide if the thought or action was passive violence or physical violence.

As the monsoon rains renewed the earth, my tree grew and grew. Both branches were heavy with leaves, but the passive side became enormous.

Soon I could see how throwing away my pencil could hurt others. More graphite would need to be mined for a new pencil. Trees would be cut down. Land would be stripped bare. Villages would be lost.

Were my wants—like the one for a new pencil—more important than the needs of others?

I saw how kicking and shoving led to rioting. I saw how violence led to more violence. How wars led to more wars.

Like the soaking
rains that turned the musty
earth lush and green, new growth
finally sprouted in me.
I was responsible for my every thought
and action, yes; but I was also responsible for the
thoughts and actions of the world. To change the world,
I needed to change myself.

As the rains trickled to an end and
the sun returned, Grandfather took my
hand. We walked amid the hustle of ashram
life: new planting, chores, prayers, work.

Grandfather had a saying;
he had said it to many, and now
he said it to me:
"Be the change you wish to see
in the world, Arun."
And with Grandfather as an example
of being the change, for himself
and others, I would.

A Note from the Authors

Arun Gandhi lived with his grandfather, Mohandas K. Gandhi, India's independence and spiritual leader, at the Sevagram ashram in India for two years—from 1946–1948, from when he was twelve until he was fourteen. I had the good fortune of hearing Arun Gandhi speak in New York City when I went to a talk he gave, hoping to heal after witnessing the terror attacks on 9/11. Arun agreed to work with me to turn his childhood stories, his unique insights and memories of his grandfather, and the impact they had on his life into books, helping me keep a promise I had made to myself after surviving that devastating day: to bring something good into the world.

Examining and understanding passive violence is not an easy task. *Be the Change* asks hard questions. But having had the opportunity to speak alongside Arun in schools, churches, book festivals, and other venues, I can tell you that it is a discussion that is already happening. It is eye opening to hear and see the reaction audiences have when Arun shares this statistic: In the United States we throw away 120 billion dollars' worth of food annually. One time, when children were asked how many people could be fed with what we waste, a child bolted to his feet and said, "A zillion."

With physical violence on the increase, we need to, as the Mahatma said, shut off its fuel supply: passive violence. How many of us waste food, or throw away tools, clothes, and toys even when they are not worn out? How many of us don't recycle? How many of us think bad things about others? About ourselves? Call people names? Judge others? If we don't want to live in a violent world, we must stop the fuel supply. And we do that, each of us, young and old, by examining and understanding our thoughts, actions, and reactions. It is only then that we can be the change we want to be for ourselves, for others, for this world.

Instinctively, children know that change is needed in the world. They want to make a difference. Collecting coins to donate, feeding the hungry, inventing technologies that benefit humanity—whatever a person's own unique tools and talents are, they can be used to be the change we want to see in this world. That's why we created the Be the Change Pledge. We hope you will not only take the pledge, but also live the pledge.

We can all be the change together. Join us.

Bethany Hegedus and Arun Gandhi

Be the Change Pledge

I pledge to dig deep to understand passive violence, to find the roots of
  my thoughts and actions.
I pledge to not overuse resources—to focus on my needs over my wants.
I pledge to learn to work with others, as one, for the good of all.
I pledge to be the change I wish to see in the world.

Visit grandfathergandhi.com for additional resources and tools.